STECK-VAUGHN
PORTRAIT OF AMERICA

Oklahoma

Steck-Vaughn Company

Executive Editor	Diane Sharpe
Senior Editor	Martin S. Saiewitz
Design Manager	Pamela Heaney
Photo Editor	Margie Foster

Proof Positive/Farrowlyne Associates, Inc.
Program Editorial, Revision Development, Design, and Production

Consultant: Oklahoma Tourism and Recreation Department, Travel & Tourism Division

Published by Raintree Steck-Vaughn Publishers, an imprint of Steck-Vaughn Company.

A Turner Educational Services, Inc. book. Based on the Portrait of America television series by R. E. (Ted) Turner.

Cover Photo: Waterfall at Turner Falls by © Richard Stockston/Southern Stock.

Library of Congress Cataloging-in-Publication Data

Thompson, Kathleen.
    Oklahoma / Kathleen Thompson.
       p.   cm. — (Portrait of America)
    "A Turner book."
    "Based on the Portrait of America television series"—T.p. verso.
    Includes index.
    ISBN 0-8114-7381-3 (library binding).—ISBN 0-8114-7462-3 (softcover)
    1. Oklahoma—Juvenile literature. I. Title. II. Series:
Thompson, Kathleen. Portrait of America.
F694.3.T48 1996
976.6—dc20

                        95-44436
                        CIP
                        AC

Printed and Bound in the United States of America

1 2 3 4 5 6 7 8 9 10 WZ 98 97 96 95

Acknowledgments
The publishers wish to thank the following for permission to reproduce photographs:
Pp. 7, 8 © Fred W. Marvel/Oklahoma Tourism & Recreation Department; p. 10 Oklahoma Archaeological Survey, University of Oklahoma; p. 11 © Fred W. Marvel/Oklahoma Tourism & Recreation Department; p. 12 Woolaroc Museum, Bartlesville, OK; pp. 13, 14 Western History Collection, University of Oklahoma Library; p. 15 (top) © Fred W. Marvel/Oklahoma Tourism & Recreation Department, (bottom) Western History Collection, University of Oklahoma Library; p. 16 (top) Oklahoma City Convention and Tourism Bureau, (bottom) Western History Collection, University of Oklahoma Library; p. 17 Western History Collection, University of Oklahoma Library; p. 18 Colorado Historical Society; pp. 20, 21 Art and Photography Courtesy Will Rogers Memorial of Claremore, Oklahoma; pp. 22, 23 Courtesy Mildred Cleghorn; p. 24 UPI/Bettmann; p. 25 Courtesy Mildred Cleghorn; p. 26 © Fred W. Marvel/Oklahoma Tourism & Recreation Department; p. 28 (top) Donek Photo, American Petroleum Institute, (bottom) © Christy Collins; p. 29 Oklahoma Wheat Commission; p. 30 © Fred W. Marvel/Oklahoma Tourism & Recreation Department; p. 32 National Cowboy Hall of Fame; p. 33 (top) Oklahoma Tourism & Recreation Department, (bottom) © Jim Argo/Oklahoma Historical Society; p. 34 © Woody Guthrie Publications; p. 35 (both) © Fred W. Marvel/Oklahoma Tourism & Recreation Department; p. 36 Courtesy Gershon and Rebecca Fenster Museum of Jewish Art; p. 37 (middle) Oklahoma City Zoological Park, (bottom) © Don Sibley/Metro Tulsa Chamber of Commerce; pp. 38, 39, 40, 41 © Fred W. Marvel/Oklahoma Tourism & Recreation Department; p. 42 © Superstock; p. 44 © Fred W. Marvel/Oklahoma Tourism & Recreation Department; p. 46 One Mile Up; p. 47 (top left) © G. Lasley/Vireo, (top right) © Gilbert Grant/Photo Researchers, (bottom) One Mile Up.

STECK-VAUGHN

PORTRAIT OF AMERICA

Oklahoma

Kathleen Thompson

A Turner Book

RSVP

RAINTREE
STECK-VAUGHN
PUBLISHERS
The Steck-Vaughn Company

Austin, Texas

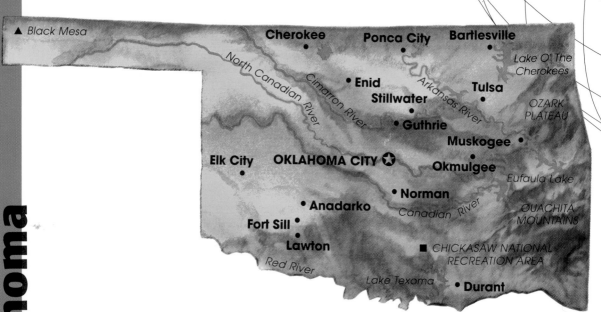

Oklahoma

▲ Black Mesa

Cherokee

Ponca City

Bartlesville

Lake O' The
Cherokees

North Canadian River

Cimarron River

Enid

Stillwater

Arkansas River

Tulsa

OZARK
PLATEAU

Guthrie

Muskogee

Elk City

OKLAHOMA CITY ☆

Okmulgee

Eufaula Lake

Norman

Canadian River

OUACHITA
MOUNTAINS

Anadarko

Fort Sill

Lawton

■ CHICKASAW NATIONAL
RECREATION AREA

Red River

Lake Texoma

Durant

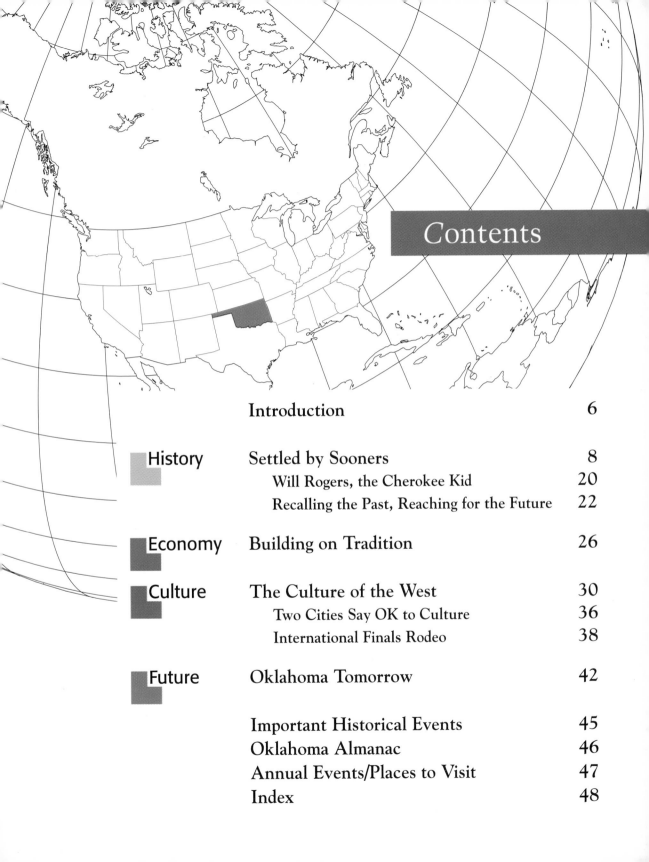

Contents

Introduction

On the front lawn of the Oklahoma state capitol building, oil pumps operate day and night. That's Oklahoma—a state of sharp contrasts united by oil. Rich forests cover about one fifth of the state, and millions of cattle graze on the wide plains of grassland and wildflowers. The Red River and the Arkansas River wind eastward, irrigating vast wheat, cotton, and vegetable farms. In the river valley, out among the crops, there's an oil pump. From the Ozark Plateau to the Gypsum Hills in the northwest, oil deposits abound. Oklahoma has sandstone ridges, steep bluffs, tumbling waterfalls, and over three hundred lakes. And, most everywhere, Oklahoma has oil!

Oklahomans celebrate the 1889 land rush during 89er Day at the Guthrie Rodeo.

Oklahoma

Settled by Sooners

Thousands of years ago, Paleo people lived in Oklahoma. Caves in the western Panhandle region contain petroglyphs, which are primitive drawings of people and animals. There is other evidence of these people, such as bone fishhooks, animal skin pouches, and even cakes made of corn and berries. About 500 B.C., Mound Builders moved into what is now Oklahoma and stayed for about a thousand years. These people built huge earthen mounds that supported homes and religious structures. Other mounds were burial sites. In these mounds archaeologists have found sculptures, metalwork, and carved bowls made from shells.

Around A.D. 1500, present-day Oklahoma became home to several Native American groups. Some of these people—Pawnee, Cheyenne, and Kiowa—followed the buffalo herds in the southern region of the Great Plains, including eastern and central Oklahoma. In the eastern section of the Oklahoma region lived the Wichita and Caddo groups. These

A Cherokee woman weaves a basket from reeds at Tsa-La-Gi Ancient Village in Tahlequah.

Native Americans made these petroglyphs at Cimarron Canyon approximately ten thousand years ago.

farming people built small villages along Oklahoma's rivers and grew crops such as corn and squash. They also fished and hunted small animals.

In 1541 Francisco Vásquez de Coronado, a Spanish explorer, came to Oklahoma from Mexico. He was searching for the Seven Cities of Cíbola. He had heard stories in Mexico about these fabulous cities of gold. Coronado didn't find the cities, so he traveled on after he had claimed the land for Spain.

A few years later, another great Spanish explorer, Hernando de Soto, came to present-day Oklahoma. He was exploring the western valleys of the Mississippi River and looking for gold. De Soto also claimed the land for Spain.

The Spanish built no settlements in Oklahoma, but they did leave something important behind—horses. Horses changed the culture of every Native American group in the West. Suddenly it was much easier to travel and to expand territory. The Cheyenne became so powerful that they pushed other Plains groups, such as the Apache, to the south and the west. Some Plains groups had warrior cultures, and the use of horses completely changed Native American warfare. Other groups, such as the Osage, saw their agricultural heritage change completely because of horses. Instead of setting up permanent farming villages, these people became nomadic hunters. They followed the migrations of the buffalo, carrying their homes and their belongings with them throughout the Great Plains.

Other influences changed the lives of Native Americans. The French had explored the Mississippi River for a long time. In 1682 René-Robert Cavelier, Sieur de La Salle, traveled down the river to the Gulf of Mexico. He and other French explorers claimed all of the land west of the Mississippi River for France. La Salle named the land the Louisiana Territory in honor of his king, Louis XIV. Now two countries—Spain and France—claimed to own the same land! They fought several wars over the next one hundred years. Finally, in 1800 Spain transferred all its claims to the Louisiana Territory to France.

The United States had won the Revolutionary War against Great Britain in 1783 and wanted to expand. So in 1803 the United States bought the Louisiana Territory for $15 million. The area we now know as Oklahoma was part of that land.

President Thomas Jefferson sent explorers to map the Oklahoma region. Captain Richard Sparks was assigned to chart the Red River, and Captain Zebulon Pike explored the Arkansas River. Americans also set up forts to defend the land from attacks by the Spanish and by Native Americans.

One major change to the Oklahoma region began on the East Coast of the United States. People in the East wanted more land, but it

Tsa-La-Gi Ancient Village in Tahlequah is a reproduction of a sixteenth-century Cherokee village. Tahlequah was established in 1839 by the Cherokee after their removal from the East.

belonged to what are called the "Five Civilized Tribes"—the Cherokee, the Chickasaw, the Creek, the Choctaw, and the Seminole. These Native American groups had already lost much of their land through treaties with settlers before and after the Revolutionary War. But the settlers wanted all of the land. In 1830 President Andrew Jackson and Congress passed the Indian Removal Act. This law ordered that the Five Civilized Tribes be given land in "Indian Territory" west of the Mississippi River in exchange for their homeland. The new territory included parts of today's Nebraska, Kansas, and Oklahoma.

The Native American groups did not want to leave. They had lived in the same place for hundreds of years. Some had added European customs to their own traditions in an effort to get along with the settlers. Over a period of about ten years, with soldiers as guards, more than one hundred thousand Native

"Trail of Tears," painted by Elizabeth Janes, depicts Native Americans of the Southeast being forced off their land and into Oklahoma in the early 1800s.

American people were forced to march through the wilderness to Oklahoma. Of the thirteen thousand Cherokee removed to Oklahoma, almost four thousand died. Other groups suffered similar losses. So many people died that the path they traveled has been called the Trail of Tears.

The pattern was repeated west of the Indian Territory. Gold was discovered in California in 1848. Settlers that headed toward the West Coast as part of the California gold rush constantly encountered Native Americans. To make sure that the routes to California stayed open, the federal government removed more and more Native Americans from their traditional lands. As early as 1850, the Caddo, the Quapaw, and the southern Apache were moved onto reservations in Indian Territory.

By the 1860s slavery was a major topic of disagreement between the southern and northern states. Finally, in 1861, eleven southern states withdrew from the Union. Shortly after, the Civil War began. The people of the Five Civilized Tribes felt they had to take sides.

The Five Civilized Tribes had more in common with the South than with the North. They had African American slaves when they had lived in the East, and they continued that way of life on plantations in the Indian Territory. They had come from the South, and many of them supported slavery, so they entered the war on the side of the Confederacy. There were Native American regiments. Stand Watie, a Cherokee, even became a general in the Confederate Army.

General Stand Watie was the only Native American brigadier general in the Confederate Army.

Confederate General Robert E. Lee surrendered to the Union Army in 1865, thus ending the Civil War. As punishment for siding with the Confederacy, the federal government greatly reduced the size of the reservations. They took away from the Indian Territory all of the land outside the present state of Oklahoma. The government also cut the size of Indian Territory within the Oklahoma region by more than half. Native Americans were even forced to allow the railroads to come through the land they were allowed to keep.

There were more Native American groups in the region all the time. In the years after the war, the government continued to move Native Americans out of the settlers' way. The Comanche, the Osage, the Wichita, and the Kiowa were put in reservations in Indian Territory. To protect settlers from Native Americans, the federal government declared that the Native Americans had to stay on the reservations all the time. They couldn't even leave the reservation to hunt for food. Their traditional lifestyle, built around the nomadic life of the Plains, came to an end.

A group of Cheyenne and Arapaho were moved from Colorado to an Oklahoma reservation in 1869. Here, they wait for their ration of beef cattle at Cantonment in 1890.

About two years after the Civil War, Texas cowboys began herding cattle north to Kansas. This was known as a cattle drive. There the cattle were herded onto trains and shipped east to cities such as Chicago and New York. The cattle drives had to pass through Oklahoma. Some cattle owners paid the Native Americans for the right to drive the cattle through and to graze them on Native American land. Between 1866 and 1885, over six million cattle passed through Oklahoma.

The Chisholm Trail was blazed by part-Cherokee trader Jesse Chisholm in 1866. Texas cowboys used the Chisholm Trail to drive cattle north to Kansas. The Chisholm Trail Festival in Yukon commemorates their efforts.

The federal government continued the policy of confining Native Americans to Indian Territory. By 1889 more than sixty Native American groups lived in the greatly reduced Indian Territory. Settlers had claimed the land that surrounded the territory, and more settlers were coming. In the middle of the territory was an area that had not yet been assigned to any Native American group. Settlers began to enter the territory to get that land. These people were called "Sooners" and "Boomers" because they had gotten to the land first. The United States Army turned the Sooners back, but the settlers' demands were too strong for the government to resist for long.

Several families await the opening of the Kiowa-Comanche and Wichita lands in 1901. These were the last Native American lands opened for a land rush.

In 1889 Congress bought three million acres of land from the Creek and the Seminole. That land was added to the open land. Announcements were published saying that people who wanted to settle there could claim all

By 1889 most of Oklahoma was occupied by Native Americans who had been removed from their ancestral lands. This historic photo shows some of the earliest settlers of Oklahoma City.

These African American homesteaders stake their claim after a land rush.

parts of this land on the morning of April 22, 1889. In preparation, the land was marked off in parcels. That morning fifty thousand homesteaders lined up on the border of the "free land." Someone fired a pistol, and the settlers were off, racing to claim their parcel. By nightfall two settlements of more than ten thousand people each had been created!

A year later the section of land that had been settled became known officially as the Oklahoma Territory. At the same time, the Panhandle region, which had been purchased earlier from Texas, was added to Oklahoma Territory.

By the turn of the century, the Oklahoma region was divided into two territories. The western half of the state, including the Panhandle, made up Oklahoma Territory. Indian Territory had been reduced to the eastern half of the area that once had belonged to the Five Civilized Tribes. Representatives of both territories worked together in a petition for statehood. In 1907 Oklahoma became the forty-sixth state. Guthrie was the first capital, and Oklahoma City became the capital in 1910.

Many farms in Oklahoma failed because the soil wasn't as rich as farmers were used to in the East. Not only did the land produce fewer crops, but the prices for farm products were so low that farmers couldn't earn a living. The land produced something else instead—oil. A settler had first discovered oil on his land in 1859. Oil wasn't drilled for commercial use until 1897, near Bartlesville in northeastern Oklahoma. Thousands of people rushed to Oklahoma to share in the newfound wealth. Oil derricks, which support the drilling mechanism, popped up anywhere there was an open piece of land. Towns grew up overnight to house the newcomers. In 1928 one of the largest oil fields in the world was discovered underneath Oklahoma City. For a while the wells of this field produced 6,500 barrels of oil a day! Many people became very rich. The wealth came to everyone. For instance, both the Osage and the Seminole became very wealthy.

In 1917 the United States entered World War I. The war had a positive effect on Oklahoma's economy because there was great demand for Oklahoma's oil and farm products. But that demand began to drop when the war ended in 1918. In the 1920s the prices for farm goods fell. Oklahoma farmers already had problems, and low prices for their goods made their situation even more difficult. Then, in the late 1920s, oil prices fell, too.

Oil refineries are a symbol of the oil boom that took place at the beginning of the twentieth century.

In the 1930s the whole country was hit by the Great Depression. Banks failed, and businesses closed. People lost their jobs, and the prices of farm products and oil dropped to almost nothing. Then, in 1933 drought hit the Great Plains. Thousands of acres of crops died because of lack of rain. Farmers had dug up the prairie sod to plant their crops. These webbed roots of prairie grasses could have held the soil in place, but now the whole region became what people called the Dust Bowl. Winds whipped the dry soil into clouds that were so high and so thick that they blocked the sun. Finally, thousands of farmers were forced to leave Oklahoma. Many went to California to find work. Many oil workers and miners also left the state.

When the drought ended, the farmers planted trees and grew crops that would hold the soil in place. Demand for Oklahoma's products—oil, beef, and wheat—increased, especially when the United States entered World War II in 1941. As wartime production increased, many people moved into the cities to work in factories and oil refineries. By the end of the war, more people worked in the cities than worked on the land.

In the 1950s the state worked hard to attract a wide variety of new industries. New road systems made it easier to ship products throughout the state and across

This farm equipment was buried in dust raised by the Dust Bowl storms. During the Dust Bowl, many families left Oklahoma for the promise of more fertile fields in California.

the country. Senator Robert Kerr of Oklahoma, with help from others, persuaded Congress to pass legislation to fund a navigation project on the Arkansas River. The project started in 1947 and was finished in 1971. Because of the McClellan-Kerr Arkansas River Navigation Project, Oklahoma products could be transported to Tulsa or Oklahoma City. Then they could be shipped to the Gulf of Mexico and from there to anywhere.

By the 1960s Oklahoma began to attract industries that produce plastics, electronics, computers, and other high-tech products. Oklahoma also became involved in aviation and the space industry. The oil and gas industry continued to grow. In the 1970s the demand for oil was great, so prices were high. But in the 1980s, the demand for these products fell drastically, and hundreds of wells were shut down. When food prices also fell, Oklahoma's economy suffered. The state relied on its other industries to help out the economy. Oklahoma also successfully attracted new industries. In the 1990s that effort continues.

One of Oklahoma's strengths is its ability to pull together in an emergency. In April 1995 the Alfred P. Murrah Federal Building in Oklahoma City was bombed. Local residents worked together with firefighters and other rescue teams to search for people missing in the destruction. Hundreds of others donated blood or brought supplies to the rescue site. In the weeks that followed, Oklahoma's dignity in the face of grief was a model for a heartsick nation.

Will Rogers, the Cherokee Kid

When Will Rogers was a boy learning how to rope cattle, furniture, and friends, he never dreamed he would be a star. The fact is he could hardly believe it when it happened. After all, when Will Rogers went on the stage, he wasn't acting. He was just being himself. And that's exactly why people loved him.

Will Rogers was born in 1879 in the Indian Territory in what is now Oklahoma. He was partly of Cherokee descent. Rogers left home to work in Texas as a cattle driver when he was 19 years old. A few years later, he also tried ranching in Oklahoma. In 1902 Rogers traveled to Argentina and then to South Africa. His career began there doing rope tricks in a Wild West show. By the time he began performing as "the Cherokee Kid," he could rope a horse and a rider at the same time, using two separate ropes. He even made it look easy!

The only problem was that it looked so easy that people sometimes forgot to be impressed. So Rogers

Referring to his Native American heritage, Will Rogers said, "My ancestors may not have come over on the Mayflower, but they met 'em at the boat."

began explaining his tricks. Then he would add, in his shy, endearing way, "that is, I'll do it if I'm lucky, and I'm not sure I will be." His audiences would roar with laughter, and they'd cheer when he did the trick right. They found themselves laughing merrily when he failed, too. Rogers used his failures as a chance to make a joke. Often, he purposely failed to jump through a rope loop, just so he could drawl, "Well, I got all my feet through but one."

Soon Rogers was more popular for his funny, good-natured remarks than he was for his horse and rope tricks. He began making wry and witty comments about politics, current events, and modern life. He wrote weekly articles, went on lecture tours, and even appeared in movies. In fact he became so loved and trusted that he was actually invited to run for President in 1928, and he was nominated as a candidate in 1932. He turned down the offers with his usual good humor. "Can't," he explained. "I look terrible in a dress suit."

As an ordinary citizen, however, Rogers was glad to offer advice and his own homespun philosophy. Audiences wanted to hear it, read it, and see it in motion pictures.

Why was Will Rogers's advice and teasing so easy to take? Perhaps because it was gentle; perhaps because it was true. More likely, however, most people understood that his comments were all in fun. They believed Will Rogers when he said with a grin, "I joked about every prominent man of my time, but I never met a man I didn't like."

In this photograph, Will Rogers does a rope trick on horseback. When he wasn't performing, the world-famous comedian found time to write six books and star in 71 movies.

Recalling the Past, Reaching for the Future

From the 1830s through the end of the century, the United States government forced many Native American groups to leave their homelands. They were moved to make room for European immigrants who wanted to settle on the land. Many of the Native American groups fought back, but they were eventually rounded up and sent to what is now Oklahoma. The Chiricahua Apache and the Cherokee are two groups of Native Americans who found themselves in Oklahoma, far from their native homes.

Until the 1870s the Chiricahua Apache lived in the territory that included present-day New Mexico, southeastern Arizona, and northern parts of Mexico. The Chiricahua were known as warriors. During the 1860s they fought fiercely to prevent the United States government from taking their land. They fought under leaders such as Cochise and Geronimo. In 1876 the United States Army forced a group of four thousand Chiricahua to move to the barren San Carlos Reservation in Arizona. Many of them fled the reservation, however, and returned to their homeland. They continued to fight for their freedom under the leadership of Geronimo.

In 1886 the Chiricahua finally lost all their territory. The United States government sent Geronimo and nearly four hundred other Chiricahua Apache to Florida, where they were held as prisoners of war. Several years later the

Mildred Cleghorn's father served as an Apache scout for federal troops.

This 1913 picture shows Apache women being forced to leave their ancestral homeland. Mildred Cleghorn's mother is circled in the photograph.

government moved the group to Alabama. In 1890 they were moved again—this time to the Fort Sill Military Reservation in Oklahoma Territory.

In 1913 the government gave the Chiricahua Apache of Fort Sill the choice of staying in Oklahoma or joining other Apache on the Mescalero Reservation in southern New Mexico. Those who preferred to remain in Oklahoma would receive sections of land to farm. Of the 239 Chiricahua remaining on the reservation, 76 decided to stay in Oklahoma as the Fort Sill Apache Tribe.

The group has worked hard to maintain a sense of their culture and history. In 1976 they adopted their own constitution. Tribal leader Mildred Cleghorn has dedicated her life to keeping Chiricahua Apache culture alive. In 1993 the group included 375 people. All were descendants of the prisoners of war.

Wilma Mankiller and other Native American leaders met with Interior Secretary Donald Hodel and President Ronald Reagan at the White House in 1988.

The Cherokee homeland is much farther away than the Chiricahua's. Since the mid-1600s, the Cherokee had lived in the Appalachian Mountain region of the southeastern United States. When European settlers arrived there in the 1700s, the Cherokee fought many battles to keep their territory. They still lost much of their land.

In the late 1700s, the Cherokee developed a form of self-government similar to that of the United States. They also began farming. A Cherokee named Sequoyah invented a syllabary, which is a writing system that uses symbols to represent spoken syllables. Because of the syllabary, a majority of Cherokee learned to read and write their own language.

In the 1800s gold was discovered on Cherokee land. The Cherokee again were in a battle with the federal government to keep settlers off of their land. In 1830 the federal government ordered all Native American groups to move west. The Cherokee refused. By

1833 other Native American groups had been removed from the area east of the Mississippi. In 1838 the United States government sent the Army to remove the remaining Cherokee. The Cherokee were forced to leave their home. Between 13,000 and 17,000 Cherokee made the journey, mostly on foot, to the Oklahoma Territory. Thousands died during the 116-day march, known as the Trail of Tears.

The Cherokee set up a partially independent government in Oklahoma Territory, known as the Cherokee Nation. About 47,000 Cherokee still live in the Cherokee Nation in north-eastern Oklahoma.

In 1985 Wilma Mankiller was named the new Principal Chief of the Cherokee Nation. She is the first woman ever to hold the office. Chief Mankiller was reelected leader of the Cherokee Nation in 1987 and again in 1991. She has increased the number of services available to the Cherokee. Chief Mankiller also has plans to develop a Cherokee language and literacy project, a health-care system, and a variety of services for children and youth. Comments she made in 1991 about her people's progress through years of difficulties can give hope to all Native American groups: "It's a fine time for celebration because as we approach the twenty-first century, the Cherokee Nation still has a strong . . . tribal government . . . that's growing and progressing and getting stronger."

Mildred Cleghorn says that she works hard to preserve Apache traditions because "We didn't want to disappear from the face of the earth and just leave . . . nothing."

Building on Tradition

Things grow in Oklahoma—wheat, cotton, peanuts. Things are taken from the ground in Oklahoma—oil, natural gas, coal. And things are made in Oklahoma—gasoline, computers, transportation equipment. This is a productive state with a productive economy.

The service industry makes up 69 percent of Oklahoma's economy. In the service industry, people do things for other people instead of making, assembling, or selling a product. The largest part of the service industry is wholesale and retail trade. Retail trade is selling products to people. Wholesale trade is selling products to stores that sell products to people. Two of the leading wholesale companies in the United States are based in Oklahoma. Flemming Companies distributes food all over the country, and Union Equity Co-op Exchange distributes grain.

The next group of service industries—government, community, and social services—makes up 15 percent of Oklahoma's economy. Government includes

This statue of a coal miner in McAlester Chadick Park honors Oklahoma's coal miners. Oklahoma is one of the leading coal producers in the nation.

Natural gas is piped from wells to users all over the country.

There are five million beef cattle in Oklahoma. They provide most of the state's income from agriculture.

workers in government offices, schools, police and fire departments, and the military. Community and social services include hospitals as well as car rental agencies and telephone companies.

Manufacturing makes up about 14 percent of Oklahoma's economy. The leading product is transportation equipment, such as automobile parts and military aircraft. Industrial plants in Oklahoma City provide equipment to the oil industry. Food processing is a growing industry that is considered manufacturing, too. For example, mills turn wheat into flour and other products.

Mining has a long tradition in Oklahoma. Today, it brings in nine percent of the state's income. Oklahoma usually ranks fourth in the country in oil production. Where there's oil, there's natural gas, and Oklahoma's natural gas production is growing. Oklahoma also has coal, iodine, limestone, and other minerals that contribute to its economy.

Agriculture is also part of Oklahoma's tradition, especially cattle ranching. Agriculture brings in about four percent of Oklahoma's economy. Livestock, such as beef cattle and chickens, brings the state twice as much money as field crops do. The biggest field crop is wheat, which is grown in the Plains area of

These workers are harvesting the state's most important crop, winter wheat.

the state. In the southwestern part of the state, farmers grow cotton. Peaches and pecans are grown in the eastern part of Oklahoma. Other crops are soybeans, hay, oats, corn, and sorghum.

Another part of Oklahoma's economy is tourism. In 1989 tourists spent $2.37 billion in Oklahoma on places to stay, meals, fishing and hunting fees, and other recreational activities. Tourists are drawn to the state by its natural and artificial lakes. Oklahoma also provides plenty of entertainment for those who like to experience the culture of Native Americans or relive some of the lifestyle of the Old West. The Plains area has dude ranches, and there are rodeos held through-out the state.

Oklahoma's economy is still developing. The people of the state know that many more sources for income are needed other than agriculture and oil. The demand for these products can rise or fall when the economy of the whole country rises or falls. The more new businesses that are attracted to Oklahoma, the more secure Oklahoma's future will be.

The Culture of the West

Oklahoma's culture reflects the way of life of many different kinds of people. Native Americans are an important part of Oklahoma's culture. Every summer the Red Earth Festival is held in Oklahoma City. Over one hundred Native American groups, including Kiowa, Pawnee, Arapaho, Cheyenne, and Cherokee, are represented at the festival. Native Americans in traditional costumes perform dances and play traditional music.

All over the state, Native American groups hold powwows that celebrate their culture. The Creek Nation Festival in Okmulgee is one example. Anadarko in the southwestern area of the state calls itself the "Indian Capital of the Nation." There you'll find bronze statues of famous Native Americans such as Sequoyah, the Cherokee who invented a writing system for the language of his people. There's also a statue of Geronimo, the Apache leader who fought many battles to keep his people free.

These covered wagons are arriving in Guthrie for the 89er Day celebration. The wagons were called prairie schooners because from a distance, their canvas tops looked like ship sails.

"The Admirable Outlaw," a painting by N. C. Wyeth, hangs in the National Cowboy Hall of Fame.

Just outside of Muskogee, in northeastern Oklahoma, is Fort Gibson Military Park. Fort Gibson was the center of activity when the Five Civilized Tribes were moved into Indian Territory. It has been preserved as a monument to that time. Muskogee has the Five Civilized Tribes Museum, which includes Native American works of art. It also includes a library of documents and rare books produced during the years of the Indian Territory.

Cowboys certainly played an important role in Oklahoma's history. This is the state to visit if you want to see some of the greatest rodeo riders in the United States. In fact some of the riders and ropers there are the best in the world. You can see examples during the International Finals Youth Rodeo and Trade Show.

Oklahoma City is the home of the National Cowboy Hall of Fame and Western Heritage Center. This museum is really a collection of museums. For example, people who worked hard on the open range are honored in the Joe Grandee Museum of the Frontier West. Another museum is dedicated to actors such as John Wayne and Gene Autry, who starred in movies about the West. Another has many paintings and sculptures by great Western artists such as Charles Russell and Frederic Remington. In still another, the spurs and saddles of the Rodeo Hall of Fame are on display. The Hall of Great Westerners honors the achievements of two hundred men and women who played important roles in the development of the West.

One day in 1889 thousands of settlers lined up at a "starting line" in central Oklahoma. A pistol shot signaled the moment when they set off to claim parcels of land that were being given away. That day is remembered every year in the Great American West Celebration. The event begins with the arrival of a wagon train, complete with pioneers in traditional clothes. The next day the land rush is reenacted. Guthrie, a town north of Oklahoma City, was created on that monumental 1889 morning. For a time it was even the capital city of Oklahoma Territory. Today, much of the city is exactly as it was when it was built. Guthrie hosts the largest 89er Day celebration in the state each year.

Life in the early trading posts is reenacted during the annual Spring Encampment. This is held at the Red River Trading Post at the Museum of the Great Plains in Lawton. Coal miners, who were an important part of Oklahoma's economy between 1870 and 1920, are honored in McCalester in southeastern Oklahoma. A monument to them has an inscription that describes the dangers and hardships of a miner's life. The inscription also praises those who "left us with an ethnic and cultural mix that has enriched us all." Another important monument is the Pioneer Woman Statue in Ponca City, in north-central Oklahoma. The statue features a proud pioneer woman walking across the prairie with her eyes straight ahead and unafraid, holding her son's hand. The monument is a memorial to the courage of all the women who met the challenges of life in early Oklahoma.

above. Ouachita National Forest is one of Oklahoma's natural wonders.

below. Bryant Baker carved the Pioneer Woman Statue, which he titled "Confident," out of a 17-foot-tall bronze block. Baker was the winner of a 1926 contest to sculpt a memorial to pioneer women.

Oklahoma legend Woody Guthrie wrote well-known songs such as "This Land Is Your Land" during the Dust Bowl days of the 1930s.

Oklahoma has had many famous citizens. Among them are two very different men—Woody Guthrie and Jim Thorpe. Guthrie was a much-beloved folksinger who wrote more than a thousand songs. Perhaps his best-known song is "This Land Is Your Land." He traveled around the country with his guitar during the 1930s. Guthrie sang and wrote songs about people during the Depression, and about the beauty of the United States and the love he felt for the country. His style and songs influenced many folksingers.

Jim Thorpe was a Native American of Sauk and Fox descent. He was a superb athlete whose career helped make professional football popular. In 1912 he became the first athlete to win both the pentathlon and decathlon Olympic events. Because he had previously received a small amount of money for playing baseball, the Olympic Committee decided he was a professional athlete and took his medals away. Many people were outraged. The Olympic Committee restored his medals in 1982, long after Thorpe's death. Sports reporters in 1950 selected Thorpe as the greatest athlete and football player in the first half of the twentieth century. In addition to professional football, he played professional baseball and excelled at swimming, basketball, boxing, lacrosse, and hockey. Thorpe also served as the first president of the American Football Association, today called the National Football League.

The fine arts also exist in Oklahoma, of course. Oklahoma City and Tulsa are the cultural centers of the state, but fine arts are represented in other cities and towns, too. There are symphony orchestras in Oklahoma City, Tulsa, Lawton, Enid, and Norman. Smaller towns support their own musical groups. And the state has produced several world-famous ballerinas, including Maria and Marjorie Tallchief and Rosella Hightower. All over the state there are writer's clubs, poetry societies, and folklore groups.

The culture of Oklahoma works both to preserve the traditions of its people and to continue moving forward. No matter what form it takes, Oklahoma's culture reflects the unique richness and vitality of the American West.

Turner Falls, near Davis, provides relaxation and beauty for Oklahoma visitors.

Tourists who visit the Gloss Mountains Conservation Area, near Orienta, come face to face with history. The mesas and red earth are exactly as they were before Europeans settled in Oklahoma.

Two Cities Say OK to Culture

The two largest cities in Oklahoma are Tulsa and Oklahoma City. Although both cities owe much of their growth to the discovery of oil, they are different places. Their differences show up in their cultures.

Tulsa emphasizes the fine arts in its museums. The Philbrook Museum of Art was once the mansion of oil "king" Waite Phillips. Today, it houses a fine collection of works from all cultures. The Gilcrease Museum has an outstanding collection of Native American art, including watercolors by Kiowa Five, noted Native American painters. The museum also has a large collection of works by famous Western artists, including Charles M. Russell, Frederic Remington, and George Catlin. Tulsa also has other specialized museums. The Greenwood historical district is the center of African American cultural history in Tulsa. It includes the Mabel B. Little Heritage Center and the Oklahoma Jazz Hall of Fame.

The culture of Oklahoma City seems more "Western" than Tulsa's. Early in its history, Oklahoma City was a major meat-processing center. Its huge meat-packing facilities, which closed in 1961, were called "Stockyards City." Today, the bustling Stockyards remains the largest cattle market in the world. This national landmark is also the site of festivals and historical reenactments. Oklahoma City is also the home of the National Cowboy Hall of Fame and Western Heritage Center. The Hall holds more than six thousand Western artifacts such as clothing, military uniforms, firearms, and Native American materials. The Hall of Fame also has one of the most impressive collections of Western fine art in the world.

Oklahoma City also celebrates Native American culture. Every

Tulsa's Gershon and Rebecca Fenster Museum of Jewish Art contains the largest collection of Judaica in the southwest United States.

year more than one hundred Native American groups gather there for the Red Earth Festival, the largest celebration of its kind in the nation. During the festival there are competitions in drumming, dancing, and traditional costumes.

The Oklahoma City Zoological Park was established in 1904, three years before Oklahoma became a state! Today, it is home to more than 2,500 animals. In one of its exhibits, three kinds of great apes—chimpanzees, Western Lowland gorillas, and Sumatran gorillas—live in settings that are as close as possible to their native habitat.

Tulsa and Oklahoma City each provide the best of the fine arts and regional culture, which celebrates life in the Old West. Taken together, Oklahoma is a place where all people can find something that expresses their particular style.

Visitors to the Oklahoma Zoo's Great EscApe exhibit are separated from the apes only by a thin, but strong, sheet of safety glass.

The Philbrook Art Center was formerly the home of Oklahoma oilman Waite Phillips.

37

International Finals Rodeo

Rodeo dates back to the late 1800s, when cowboys used their ranching skills to compete against one another. Since then rodeos have remained popular attractions. The International Pro Rodeo Association (IPRA) has been holding the annual International Finals Rodeo in Oklahoma City since 1991. Thousands of people have gone to Oklahoma City to witness the excitement, and thousands more watch the championship on television.

The judges at the Finals are rodeo professionals. They know the rules of each rodeo event. They rate the riders and the animals, and they watch the timing clock. People known as stock contractors own and supply the animals working on the rodeo. "Stock" is rodeo talk for the cattle and the horses that the contestants will be trying to ride, rope, and wrestle. Only

Opening ceremonies at Elk City's Rodeo of Champions are always festive.

This woman is barrel riding in Guymon's Pioneer Days Rodeo. Judges will penalize her by adding five seconds to her time for any barrel she knocks over.

the best bucking horses, called "broncs," and the best cattle from the 52-member rodeo companies are brought to the Finals to challenge the riders. The contractors are responsible for following a long list of regulations to ensure the animals are healthy and well treated. Since an eight- or ten-second ride is a long ride at the rodeo, these valuable animals "work" no more than about five minutes in an entire rodeo season.

Only at the IPRA Finals can women compete with men in rodeo under the same set of rules in the six standard contest events. All the cowboys and cowgirls riding in the rodeo must qualify to participate in the Finals. To do this, they compete in a number of smaller IPRA rodeos all year long. They earn their chance to compete at the Finals by being among the top 15 moneymakers in their chosen events. Winners at the Finals are considered world champions.

There are seven different events at the Finals, with one of them being a "women's only" event. Three events are called "rough stock" events because they involve riding an untamed animal that the contestant has never seen before. The rough stock events are bareback bronc riding, saddle bronc riding, and bull riding.

Bareback riding requires riders to stay on a kicking, bucking horse for eight seconds. The riders have no saddle, stirrups, or reins, and must hold on with one hand to a strap encircling the horse behind its shoulders. Riders are disqualified if they touch the horses, themselves, or the equipment with their free hands. They

In saddle bronc riding, spurs are worn on the rider's heels to make the horse buck. This man is riding in Elk City's Rodeo of Champions.

ing, kicking bull. Hanging onto a leather strap with one hand is difficult. Falling off can be deadly. Luckily, every rodeo has rodeo clowns who have the job of attracting the wild bull's attention while the fallen rider scrambles to safety.

In the other four rodeo events, contestants ride their own highly trained horses. In steer wrestling and team roping, two riders work as partners. Steer wrestling, once called "bulldogging," was introduced to the rodeo in 1907 by Bill Pickett, an African American cowboy. The two riders are called the wrestler and the hazer. The hazer's job is to ride at a charging steer so it runs in a straight line. The wrestler jumps off his horse and grabs the steer by the horns. This is called the catch. The wrestler must stop the steer and get it flat on the ground with all four feet pointed in the same direction. The best steer-wrestling teams can get a steer to the ground in under five seconds!

are also disqualified if their boots don't stay above the horses' shoulders. Even for only eight seconds, this is no easy way to ride a wild horse.

Saddle bronc riding is the rodeo's oldest event. It began when cowboys had to tame, or "break," wild horses so they could be used for ranching and riding. Saddle bronc riding is like bareback riding except the riders use saddles. Riders must hold on with only one of their hands and keep their feet in the saddle's stirrups.

In bull riding, a rider takes a quick trip on a two-thousand-pound snort-

In team roping, riders are called the header and the heeler. In this event a seven-hundred-pound steer is released, and the header must chase it and throw a rope loop around its neck, head, or horns. The header then tugs the steer into position for the heeler. The heeler ropes the steer's back legs. All this happens in about six seconds.

Calf roping comes from the working rancher's job of rounding up calves for branding. In this event riders must chase calves and rope them. Then, as their horses pull the rope tight, the riders jump down, throw the calves to the ground, and tie three of the calves' legs together. The tie must hold for six seconds after the riders get back on their horses.

Barrel racing is a women's rodeo event. This is where the cowgirls race their horses in a cloverleaf pattern around three barrels. The turns are tight, the riding is lightning quick, and there is a penalty for any barrel knocked over. Riders must complete this race in under 17 seconds.

Rodeo is truly a sport like no other. At the International Finals Rodeo, you will see the best cowboys and cowgirls in the world give you the ride of a lifetime.

A rider prepares to rope a calf at the Creek Nation Rodeo in Okmulgee. In the calf roping rodeo event, teamwork between the horse and rider is very important.

Oklahoma Tomorrow

Oklahoma's past is full of energy, and its present is full of growing pains. Its task now is to prepare for its future. There are challenges yet to be met, and Oklahomans are preparing to do just that.

For many years Oklahoma's economy depended on agriculture and oil. That has changed as the state has attracted other sources of income, but the state still has a way to go. There are strong reasons for businesses to locate here. Oklahomans are hard workers. The state has a bounty of natural resources, and it has a well-developed transportation system. Industries need such things to prosper. It is expensive to purchase and transport raw materials from their origin to the place where they are needed. Oklahoma is working hard to improve its schools and prepare even more of its citizens for new, high-tech businesses.

Oklahoma also is changing an unproductive pattern. For a long time, the state produced raw products such as oil, beef cattle, and wheat. Those products were sent out of state to be prepared for markets. For

This sculpture of an oil pump in Oklahoma City symbolizes the creativity that will be required of industries in the future, as they learn to use resources more conservatively.

example, Oklahoma's oil is made into gasoline in other states. Now Oklahoma is developing its own processing facilities. That will help Oklahoma make more money from its raw materials.

At the same time, there are problems. There are still pockets of poverty and unemployment, especially in Native American communities. It is often difficult for Native Americans to join the state's economy without giving up some of their traditions. But the state government and the Native Americans are working together on the problem. With their energy and will, they'll find the answers that will benefit both.

Today, most Oklahomans live in cities, not in rural areas. That means that there are great pressures on cities to provide public services, such as police, fire, health, and transportation. At the same time, it is difficult to raise the money necessary to provide these services. In fact, in 1992 voters amended the state constitution in order to limit the power of the state government to raise taxes. Meeting the state's needs will take all of the creativity of Oklahoma's people. It is a challenge they are sure to meet.

The American Indian Exposition is held in Anadarko. The exposition helps preserve Oklahoma's rich Native American heritage.

Important Historical Events

1541 Fransisco Vásquez de Coronado reaches Oklahoma while looking for gold. Hernando de Soto follows. Both claim the area for Spain.

1682 René-Robert Cavelier, Sieur de La Salle, claims Oklahoma for France as part of the Louisiana Territory.

1802 Pierre Chouteau, Jr., a Frenchman, establishes a fur-trading post in present-day Salina.

1819 The Five Civilized Tribes are removed to Oklahoma along the Trail of Tears.

1820 The Choctaw are assigned land in Oklahoma by the Treaty of Doak's Stand.

1821 Sequoyah completes the Cherokee alphabet after 12 years of work.

1824 Fort Gibson is built near the mouth of the Grand (Neosho) River. Fort Towson is laid out on the Red River.

1830 Congress passes the Indian Removal Act to move eastern Native Americans to Oklahoma (Indian Territory).

1842 Fort Washita is established on the Washita River.

1850 The Texas-Oklahoma border is made final.

1854 The Oklahoma-Kansas border is fixed at the 37th parallel.

1861 The Civil War begins. Native American soldiers from Indian Territory join in the conflict.

1866 Large sections of Indian Territory are taken away from the Five Civilized Tribes as punishment for fighting on the Confederate side.

1867 Cattle drives begin from Texas, through Oklahoma Indian Territory, and end at Kansas railroad depots.

1868 Camp Wichita (Fort Sill) is founded.

1889 Fifty thousand Sooners claim unassigned land in Indian Territory.

1890 Oklahoma Territory is officially established—an island of settlement in the middle of Indian Territory.

1897 The first commercial oil well is opened near Bartlesville.

1901 Kiowa-Comanche and Wichita lands are opened to settlement.

1905 The Five Civilized Tribes call a constitutional convention and adopt a constitution for the state of Sequoyah. Congress rejects statehood.

1907 Oklahoma Territory and Indian Territory enter the Union together as the state of Oklahoma.

1910 The state capital is moved to Oklahoma City.

1928 The Oklahoma City oil fields are opened.

1930 The Great Depression begins, combining with the Dust Bowl to cause a decade of terrible hardship.

1940 Pensacola Dam on Grand (Neosho) River forms the Lake o' the Cherokees. The Denison Dam on Red River forms Lake Texoma, built in 1943.

1965 The National Cowboy Hall of Fame and Western Heritage Center is dedicated in Oklahoma City.

1982 Penn Square Bank of Oklahoma collapses. This bank failure is considered to be the costliest in United States history.

1995 The Alfred P. Murrah Federal Building in Oklahoma City is bombed, claiming 168 lives.

The flag shows an Osage shield with seven eagle feathers. The shield is crossed by two peace symbols: a peace pipe and an olive branch.

OKLAHOMA

Oklahoma Almanac

Nickname. The Sooner State

Capital. Oklahoma City

State Bird. Scissortailed flycatcher

State Flower. Mistletoe

State Tree. Redbud

State Motto. *Labor Omnia Vincit* (Labor Conquers All)

State Song. "Oklahoma"

State Abbreviations. Okla. (traditional); OK (postal)

Statehood. November 16, 1907, the 46th state

Government. Congress: U.S. senators, 2; U.S. representatives, 6. State Legislature: senators, 48; representatives, 101. Counties: 77

Area. 69,919 sq mi (181,089 sq km), 18th in size among the states

Greatest Distances. north/south, 230 mi (370 km); east/west, 464 mi (747 km)

Elevation. Highest: 4,973 ft (1,516 m). Lowest: 287 ft (87 m)

Population. 1990 Census: 3,157,604 (18% increase over 1980), 28th in size among the states. Density: 45.2 persons per sq mi (17.4 persons per sq km). Distribution: 67% urban, 33% rural. 1980 Census: 3,025,266

Economy. *Agriculture*: wheat, cotton, peanuts, soybeans, sorghum grain, barley oats, beef cattle. *Manufacturing*: nonelectrical machinery, oil field machinery, petroleum and coal products, fabricated metal products. *Mining*: petroleum, natural gas, coal, crushed stone, sand, gravel

State Bird: Scissortailed flycatcher

State Flower: Mistletoe

Annual Events

★ Cimarron Territory Celebration in Beaver (April)

★ Pioneer Days in Guymon (May)

★ Red Earth Festival of the Indian in Oklahoma City (June)

★ World Championship Watermelon Seed Spittin' Contest in Paul's Valley (June)

★ American Indian Exposition in Anadarko (August)

★ Bluegrass Music Festival in Hugo (August)

★ State Fair of Oklahoma in Oklahoma City (September)

State Seal

Places to Visit

★ Black Mesa State Park, near Kenton

★ Cherokee Heritage Center, near Tahleguah

★ Creek Capital in Okmulgee

★ Dinosaur Quarry, near Kenton

★ Fort Sill, near Lawton

★ National Cowboy Hall of Fame and Western Heritage Center in Oklahoma City

★ Ouachita National Forest, near Heavener

★ Washita Battlefield, near Cheyenne

★ Will Rogers Memorial in Claremore

★ Woolaroc Museum, near Bartlesville

Index